Pains and Strains

Dr. Alvin Silverstein,

Virginia Silverstein, and

Laura Silverstein Nunn

My Health

Franklin Watts

A Division of Scholastic Inc.

New York • Toronto • London • Auckland • Sydney

Mexico City • New Delhi • Hong Kong

Danbury, Connecticut

Photographs © 2003:Corbis Images: 11 (Philip James Corwin), 36 (Laura Dwight), 29 (Patricia McDonough); Custom Medical Stock Photo: 9; Peter Arnold Inc.: 4, 13, 18 (Jodi Jacobson), 24 (SIU, School of Medicine); Photo Researchers, NY: 8, 23 (John Bavosi/SPL), 37 (Tim Davis), 6 (GrantPix), 27 (Susie Leavines), 33 (Carolyn A. McKeone), 21 (J. Gerard Smith), 17 (Gerard Vandystadt); PhotoEdit: 40 (Richard Hutchings), 31 (Michael Newman), 25 (Nancy Sheehan), 7, 15, 16 (David Young-Wolff); The Image Works: 12 (Stuart Cohen), 26 (David Grossman), 35 (Kathy McLaughlin); Visuals Unlimited: 22 (Jeff Greenberg), 19 (D. Yeske).

Cartoons by Rick Stromoski

Library of Congress Cataloging-in-Publication Data

Silverstein, Alvin.
    Pains and Strains / by Dr. Alvin Silverstein, Virginia Silverstein, and Laura Silverstein Nunn.
        p. (cm).—(My Health)
    Includes bibliographical references and index.
    Contents: What a pain! — Body in motion — Sprains and strains — What good is pain? — Find out what's wrong — Treating pains and strains — Keep your body fit.
    ISBN 0-531-12174-7 (lib. bdg.)   0-531-16237-0 (pbk.)
    1. Sprains—Juvenile literature. 2. Overextension injuries—Juvenile literature. 3. Pain—Juvenile literature. [1. Wounds and injuries. 2. Sprains. 3. Human physiology. 4. Pain.] I. Title: Pains and Strains. II. Silverstein, Virginia B. III. Nunn, Laura Silverstein. IV. Title. V. Series.
RD106.S56 2003
617.1'7—dc21   2002011295

Contents

What a Pain!

You invite a few friends over to play a game of kick ball in your backyard. As the ball comes in your direction, you quickly run up to kick it. Suddenly, you trip over a rock hidden in the grass. Your foot turns, and you lose your balance. You land hard on the ground. When you try to get up—ow! Your ankle hurts so much you can't put any weight on it.

What's wrong? Did you break a bone? It's probably just a sprain. Sprains and strains and other painful injuries often happen during sports and other physical activities. They can also happen in a fall in your house, or when you slip on a patch of ice. Twisting your leg the wrong way or using an arm to break your fall can really hurt.

Believe it or not, pain is actually a good thing. It lets you know that something is

Did You Know...

In the United States, about 3 million children up to the age of 14 are hurt each year in sports and other play activities.

◄ **A fall can be very painful, even if you don't break any bones.**

5

wrong inside your body. When you are feeling pain, you should stop what you're doing and get help right away, before the problem gets worse.

Sprains and strains can be very painful, but they are not usually serious. These kinds of injuries can usually be treated at home, although you may need to see a doctor to make sure no bones are broken. Getting hurt can be a real pain, but there are lots of things that you can do to play it safe and avoid injury.

What are sprains and strains all about? What's the difference between the two? How do you treat them, and what can you do to prevent them? Read on to find out.

A sprained knee may hurt a lot, but it will heal over time.

Body In Motion

Whenever you move your body—whether you raise your hand, take a step, or blink your eyes—you are using your muscles. **Muscles** are bundles of many long, stretchy "threads," or **muscle fibers**. They move your hands, feet, and other body parts by pulling on the bones that make up your **skeleton**. The skeleton gives your body support. Without it, you would just be a blob.

You use at least one set of muscles every time you move.

This knee joint connects the two leg bones.

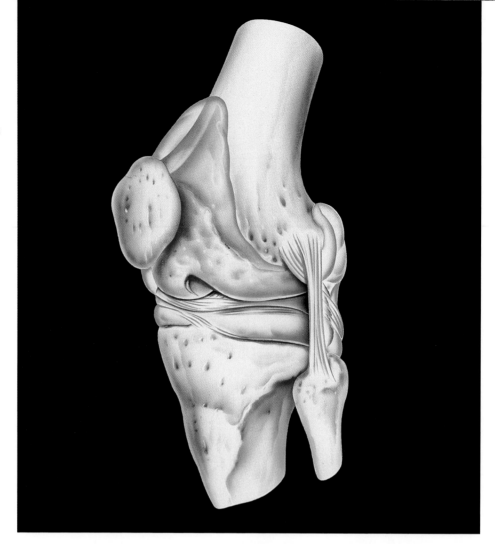

Your bones are connected by **joints**, which allow you to bend and move. The main joints are in the shoulders, elbows, wrists, hips, knees, knuckles, and ankles. The end of each bone is covered with a cushion of tough, rubbery **cartilage**. Cartilage helps to keep the bones from rubbing against each other. Without cartilage, the ends of the bones would wear away.

Strong bands of tissue called **ligaments** hold bones together in the joints. They help to keep the ends of the bones from slipping out of place. Ligaments do not stretch, but they can bend enough to allow bones to move without coming apart.

Muscle power makes your body move. Muscles are like strong rubber bands that can stretch and **contract** (tighten). They usually work in pairs. The muscles on one side of the bone contract, while the ones on the other side relax and lengthen. When you "make a muscle," the biceps (the big muscle on

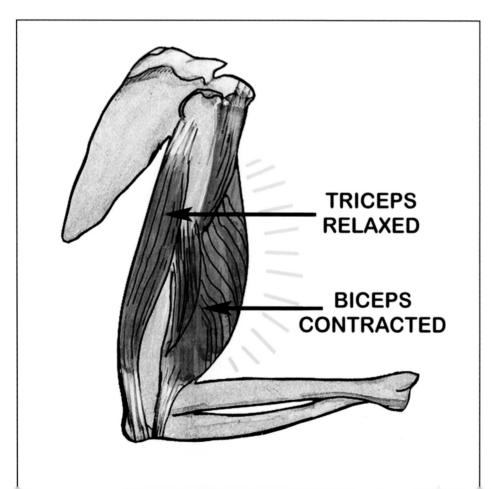

TRICEPS
RELAXED

BICEPS
CONTRACTED

You use both your biceps and triceps to make a muscle in your arm.

There are more than 650 muscles in your body. About half your body weight is muscle.

the inside of your arm) contracts to pull on the bones in your upper arm. When you straighten your arm, the biceps relaxes, while a muscle on the outside of your upper arm—the triceps—contracts to pull the arm bones out straight.

Muscles work hard, and they use a lot of energy when they contract. The muscle fibers use fuel (sugar from the food we eat) and oxygen (from the air we breathe) to produce energy. They get sugar and oxygen from the blood, which flows through a network of tiny **blood vessels**. These thin tubes reach every part of the body. Their walls are so thin that sugar and oxygen can leak out and enter the muscle fibers.

Working muscles produce waste products, including carbon dioxide. Carbon dioxide is a chemical that forms when muscles "burn" sugar for energy. These waste products pass out of the muscle fibers and into the blood vessels, and the blood carries them away.

Although many muscles pull on bones, they are not attached to bones directly. Muscles are connected to bones by tough, cordlike tissues called **tendons**. The muscle pulls on the tendon, and the tendon, in turn, pulls on the bone. Tendons are very strong tissues. They can stand up to the daily pulling and tugging as we use our muscles. You can get an idea of what tendons look like by checking out the back of your hand as you move your fingers up and down. The tendons are the long, stringy bands that run from your fingers to your wrist.

Look at the back of your hand to see the tendons that run from your fingers to your wrist.

Sprains and Strains

Your daily activities—walking, running, jumping, throwing, and carrying heavy loads—can put a lot of pressure and stress on your body. Usually, our bodies are sturdy enough to handle the pressures we place upon them day after day. But sometimes, things can go wrong. Too much stress on the body can damage muscles, ligaments, or tendons. Falling down or twisting an arm or leg the wrong way can also cause problems.

Many injuries occur when we are doing something physical, such as running, dancing, or playing sports. These are the times when we put the most stress on our bodies. Sprains and strains are the most common types of sports injuries.

Many everyday activities put stress on your bones and joints.

People often confuse sprains and strains. However, they are different kinds of injuries. A sprain occurs when a ligament is overstretched or torn. For example, sprains often happen when people break their fall and land on an outstretched arm, injuring a wrist.

Putting your arm out in front of you to break a fall may do more harm than good.

Turning or twisting a foot or leg the wrong way can overstretch or tear the ligaments in your knee and ankle joints. Getting tackled in football or stepping on something unstable, such as a ball, can turn the foot suddenly and tear the ligaments in the ankle. Ankle sprains are actually the most common injuries in sports.

When a joint is sprained, it quickly swells up as fluid leaks out of the blood vessels into the damaged tissue. The sprained joint feels hot, and it is very difficult and painful to move it. If you sprain your ankle or knee, it may be especially painful to put weight on it. You are unable to walk normally and may limp as you try to take weight off the sprained joint.

A strain, often called a pulled muscle, occurs when a muscle or tendon is overstretched or torn. This problem usually happens when too much tension is placed on the muscle. A strain may occur

Sometimes running a long race may make muscles too tired and cause injury.

when muscles are overused (running a long race) or overstretched (reaching for something that's too far).

Strains, like sprains, cause pain and swelling. Depending on how much of the muscle or tendon is damaged, a strain may be mild or serious. The muscle feels weak and painful when you try to use it.

Many people strain their back muscles. The back muscles have to work very hard to support your body every time you move, sit, or stand. When you sit or stand for too long, the muscles in the back become overused and strained. Then, your back starts to hurt. Carrying a heavy backpack can also strain back muscles, especially if it is not well balanced. Many kids carry around as much as 20 pounds (9 kilograms) every single day. That's a lot of extra stress on the back muscles.

Hamstring pulls are common sports injuries. Hamstring muscles are at the back of the upper legs. The legs have to hold up the weight of your whole body. When a person walks or runs, each leg takes turns holding up all that weight

A heavy backpack may strain your back muscles.

on its own. A hamstring strain can occur when the muscles are overloaded or they move too fast, too soon. For instance, a baseball player who makes a quick dash from one base to another is at risk for pulling a hamstring. So are sprinters—athletes who run very fast for short distances.

The calf muscles are among the strongest muscles of the body. These muscles are at the back of the lower legs, between the knee and the heel. When you leap and jump, a tremendous amount of force suddenly presses down on your lower legs.

This runner has well-developed hamstring and calf muscles.

The calf muscles can handle a force of more than a ton! But even these powerful muscles can be injured. Calf strains are most common in sports that involve a lot of jumping and stop-start movements, such as tennis, volleyball, and basketball. The calf muscles may become overstretched and torn when you stop suddenly, plant a foot firmly on the ground, and quickly straighten your knee.

Two for One

If you've got a sprain, you might get a strain too. Sometimes, sprains lead to strains. Let's say you've sprained your right ankle. That joint is a little wobbly, so your body automatically tries to give you a firmer leg to walk on by tensing the calf and thigh muscles. All the extra stress strains these muscles. Meanwhile, your ankle hurts so much when you put your weight on it that you may put extra pressure on your other leg. So the muscles of your left leg may get strained too.

Be careful not to injure your healthy leg while your injured leg heals.

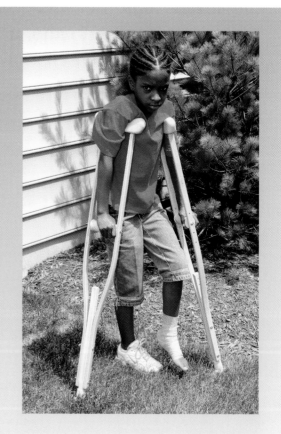

Many strains happen as a result of a single event. But some strains develop over a long period of time. These kinds of problems are known as **repetitive strain injuries** or **RSI**. RSI may develop when a person stays in an awkward position for a long time; performs the same action over and over; or does not take any time to relax during physical activities. People who use computers may spend many hours at a time with their wrists bent over a keyboard. This situation can lead to **carpal tunnel syndrome**. The tendons running through long, narrow openings in the wrist bones

Carpal tunnel syndrome may be caused by frequent typing on a keyboard.

become swollen and press on the nerves that pass through the same "tunnels." Then the hands become painful and stiff, and the fingers may feel numb. Playing video games for too long without a break can also lead to RSI. The body parts most often affected are the fingers, hands, wrists, elbows, arms, shoulders, back, and neck.

Almost everybody gets a **muscle cramp** at one time or another. During a muscle cramp, the muscles contract uncontrollably and can cause a lot of pain. Cramps occur most often in the calf or foot and may be caused by straining the muscles, overusing the muscles, or staying in the same position for too long. You can get muscle cramps while you're playing sports, exercising, or even lying down in bed. Nighttime cramps may happen after the day's busy activities. A muscle cramp or strain in the front of the thigh is sometimes called a charley horse.

Another kind of muscle injury that can occur during sports or in a fall is a **bruise**. A bruise happens when the muscles are torn by a direct blow. The torn muscles bleed, but the blood doesn't leak out of the body as it does in a cut or scrape. The blood stays under the skin and produces the blues, purples, and yellows of a "black-and-blue" mark. Over a period of days, the colors gradually fade as roaming white blood cells, the body's cleanup squad, move into the injured tissue. The extra fluid that produces swelling makes it easier for these white cells to move. They gobble up bits of damaged cells and colored chemicals that spilled out of the torn blood vessels.

A bruise is caused by blood trapped under the skin.

What Is Pain Good For?

Nobody likes the feeling of pain when they hurt themselves—whether you fall off your bike and skin your knee or twist your ankle during a soccer game. We usually think of pain as a bad thing, but actually it can be good for us. Pain acts as a warning that damage is being done to your body—or may be done unless you get help right away.

The pain you feel when you fall off your bike may be warning you that something is wrong with your body.

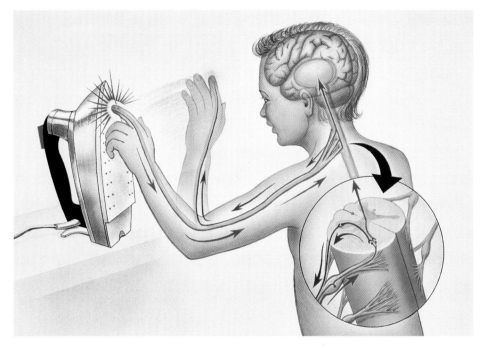

How does your body know when it's hurt? How does pain work? When you are hurt, the chemicals from damaged tissue act on special nerves that have branches reaching to nearly all parts of the body. These nerves send messages to the brain, and that's when you feel pain. Sometimes, your blood vessels swell up and put pressure on the surrounding nerves, causing more pain. Or muscles may tighten and press on nerves.

How strong the pain feels depends on the type of injury, how much damage there is, and how your body handles pain. A skinned knee may not bother

23

you very much. But the same kind of injury may cause your friend to cry out in pain. Some pains are strong and sharp, while others are dull and annoying. A dull pain that goes on for a long time may be called an ache.

Various drugs can relieve pain. Pain-relieving drugs are called **analgesics**. How do they work? When body cells or tissues are damaged, they release special chemicals. These chemicals trigger nearby nerves, which send pain messages to the brain, telling you where it hurts. Analgesics such as aspirin, acetaminophen, and ibuprofen work by stopping the cells

Aspirin and other pain relievers may help you to feel better when you have a sprain or strain.

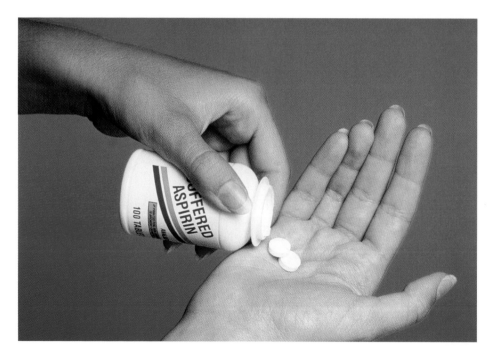

from releasing these chemicals or stopping the brain from getting the pain messages. Aspirin, ibuprofen, and naproxen also help to shrink swollen tissue, which reduces the pressure on pain nerves. Acetaminophen works only on pain, not on swelling.

Analgesics don't help to heal the injury that's causing the pain, but they can help to make you feel more comfortable. They work for only a few hours, and then the pain comes back. You shouldn't take pain medications unless your parents or doctor says so. Taking too much of a drug, or taking the wrong kind, can be harmful.

To be healthy again, you need to find out what is causing the pain and do the right things to treat it.

Natural Painkillers

Your body makes its own natural painkillers, called **endorphins**. These chemicals keep the brain from receiving pain messages and make you feel good. A good exercise workout can produce large amounts of endorphins.

Exercise releases chemicals from the brain that make you feel good.

Finding Out What's Wrong

How do you know when you have a sprain or a strain? What if it's a broken bone? If you feel pain during an activity or after a fall, don't ignore it. Remember, pain is a warning that there's something wrong. You need to stop what you're doing and pay attention. If you can't move a body part, or it hurts to put pressure on it, go to a doctor.

The first thing a doctor will do is gather information about your injury. Where does it hurt? When did it happen? What were you doing when it started to hurt? The doctor will gently touch the injured area to see if it is swollen and tender. If you hurt your ankle,

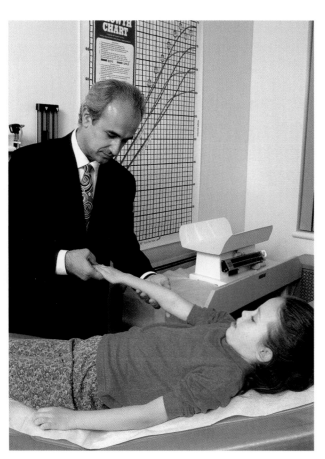

A doctor will examine your injury to determine how serious it is.

26

you may be asked to try to stand on it. Or if it's your wrist, to try to move it and pick up an object.

There are a few tests that can help to diagnose or identify the problem. An X ray may be taken to rule out a broken bone or other injury to the bone. But X rays cannot show damage to muscles, ligaments, or tendons—only to bones.

Further tests may include an MRI (magnetic resonance imaging) and ultrasound. These tests can provide images that are much more detailed. They also show details of soft tissues that an ordinary X ray cannot pick up.

MRI can show muscles, tendons, and ligaments as well as cartilage and blood vessels. It is especially good for looking at the joints, such as the knee, ankle, or wrist. MRI scans can show tears or other damage.

An MRI scan allows doctors to find any damaged tissue, muscles, or ligaments.

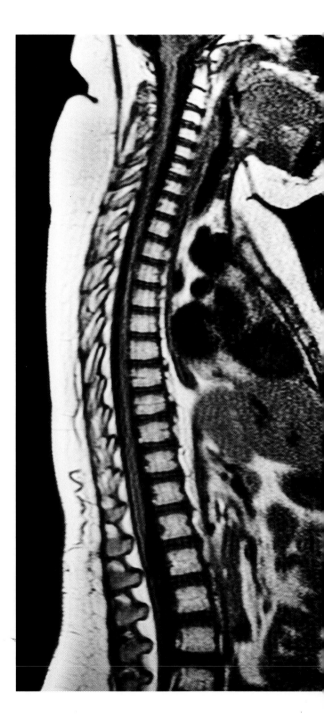

Ultrasound uses high-pitched sound waves, too high for humans to hear, to form a picture of the soft tissues. It is very good for diagnosing tendon problems.

Sometimes, pain and swelling in a joint may not be due to an injury but to a condition called **arthritis**. The joint is stiff, and it may be hot and red, too. Arthritis is a very common problem among older people. It is most often caused by years of wear on the joints that makes the cartilage covering the ends of the bones get thin. It can also occur in young people, even young children. Sometimes, it may be the result of a problem in the body's defense system, which mistakenly attacks some of the body's own tissue instead of disease germs. Arthritis may also be a symptom of Lyme disease, caused by a germ that is spread by tick bites. X rays and special blood tests can determine whether a joint problem is due to an injury or to arthritis.

Have you ever been in a car accident? Even people wearing seat belts may be bruised and shaken up when a moving car suddenly collides with something. Injuries to the neck muscles (called whiplash injuries) are especially likely because the head and neck are rapidly thrown back and forth, like the lash of a whip. Symptoms such as pain and stiffness in the neck, jaw, or shoulders; dizziness; headaches; and numbness in the arms or hands may appear right away. More often they are not noticed until hours, days, or even weeks after the accident.

A seatbelt will not protect you from whiplash.

Sometimes, pain and stiffness may develop because the neck muscles contract at the time of the accident, to protect the neck bones. These muscles get tired and sore, which makes you feel like you have been injured. So you hold your neck stiffly to keep

About 1 million whiplash injuries occur in the United States each year. Most of them happen in car, truck, or motorcycle accidents, but they can also occur in collisions in contact sports, in horseback riding, and in diving.

your head from moving and to avoid more pain. Soon, tensing the neck muscles becomes a habit.

Diagnosing whiplash injuries as soon as possible is important. When treatment is started early, the injury will heal faster. Often, though, it is very difficult to diagnose whiplash. Usually, doctors make the diagnosis from the patient's symptoms and information on the kind of accident. X rays and MRI scans can show whether there is damage to the neck bones or the cartilage cushions between them.

Doctors used to tell patients with whiplash to wear a special collar to keep the neck stable. Now they realize that this can make the pain and stiffness last longer. Gentle exercises and a gradual return to normal activities can help patients to recover faster.

Treating Sprains and Strains

The treatment for pains and strains is basically the same. Just remember the word RICE. This word may sound like a food, but it actually stands for Rest, Ice, Compression, Elevation. These are four important things you need to do for a sprain or strain—and you can do them at home.

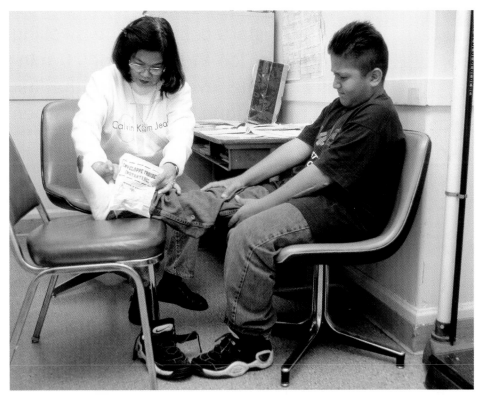

Rest, ice, compression, and elevation are the best ways to treat a sprain or strain.

Rest: Rest the injured part of the body for the first few days. Use a sling to support a sprained wrist or crutches to keep weight off a hurt knee or ankle. As the pain lessens, gradually use the injured part. Too much rest can weaken the muscles.

Ice: Place an ice pack on the injured area. Ice helps to reduce the pain and swelling. Ice the injury as soon as possible. It works best if it is started before the swelling develops. Ice the injury for 20 minutes at a time, every hour for the first twenty-four hours (except when you're sleeping).

Compression: Compress (squeeze) the injured body part for at least two days to reduce swelling. Wrap the injured part with an elastic bandage to support it and keep it from moving. Do not wrap the bandage too tightly, though, or the blood will be unable to reach this area.

Elevation: Keep the injured body part above the level of the heart for the first twenty-four hours, as much as possible, to reduce swelling.

Ice or Heat?

Sometimes, people are confused about whether to put ice or heat on a sprain or strain. As you know, ice is the key. Ice reduces pain and swelling. Heat, on the other hand, can actually increase pain and swelling. But it is okay to use a heating pad or soak in a hot bath to soothe aching muscles twenty-four hours after the injury.

Ice is a great way to reduce the pain and swelling of an injury.

Activity 1: Wrap It Up!

Do you know how to wrap a sprained ankle or knee? For this activity, you need an elastic bandage.

For an ankle sprain, start by wrapping a circle of bandage around the middle of your foot, leaving the toes bare. Pull the bandage across the top of your foot to the opposite side and around the back of your ankle. Draw the bandage down across the top of your foot to the opposite side, making an X, and circle around under the foot, about a 1/2 inch (1 cm) closer to your ankle. Continue wrapping, crossing back and forth, until you have your foot and ankle covered.

For a knee sprain, loop a circle of bandage around your lower leg, below the knee. Then bring the bandage across the back of your knee and upward to just above the knee. Loop another circle around your upper leg, and pull the bandage downward across the front of your knee. Now pull the bandage around the back and upward across the front of your knee, making an X. Make another figure eight overlapping the first one. After you have two complete figure eights, wrap around your leg in an upward spiral.

If the pain is really bothering you, you can take acetaminophen, ibuprofen, or another painkiller to make you more comfortable. For more serious sprains and strains, the doctor may need to prescribe a stronger drug that helps to reduce pain and swelling.

Massage can help to soothe sore muscles. Rubbing the injured area can help to reduce swelling because it helps to move the fluids that leaked out of the tissue back into the bloodstream. Massage also increases the flow of blood to the area, bringing nutrients that will help the injured tissues to heal. Don't overdo it, though. Rubbing too hard can damage the tissue even more and make them bleed.

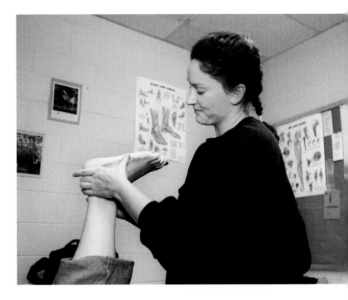

Massage is often used to treat sore muscles.

After a sprain or strain, the muscles become weak and the joints get stiff. Exercise can help your body move normally again. Your doctor can recommend exercises that are best for your particular injury. You have to start slowly, though, doing simple movements for short periods of time. If you try to do too much, you may strain your muscles all over again. This is a gradual process.

Your body
works to heal
your injuries
while you are
sleeping.

Most strains take about a week to heal completely. But sprains can take three or four weeks, or even longer, to heal. A sprained ankle can take a long time to heal because it is being used much of the time. It is important to get plenty of sleep while your injury heals. The body does most of the work of repairing damaged tissues while you are sleeping.

Surgery may be needed to repair very bad sprains or strains, especially those involving torn tendons or ligaments. For instance, a knee may need surgery after a football or skiing accident. Baseball pitchers may need surgery for damage to the rotator cuff, a band of muscles and tendons around the shoulder joint. Most sprains and strains, however, heal on their own.

Keeping Your Body Fit

Although most sprains and strains occur during sports or exercise, that doesn't mean that you should avoid physical activity. In fact, staying active helps to keep your body strong and healthy, which, in turn, helps to protect you from injuries. Even if you are injured, your body will heal faster if it is strong and healthy to begin with.

You can't just start an activity or exercise without some preparation. If your body has been resting, such as after a long night's sleep, the muscles are cold and tight. You have to loosen them up and warm them before they can work well. You can do this by doing

It is very important to stretch your muscles before you exercise.

Activity 2: Stretch Your Body

Stretching exercises can help muscles to become more **flexible** so that you can move and bend better. Do each set of exercises 10 times.

- Back Stretches:

  Lie on your back and bring one of your knees to your chest. Hold. Repeat with the other knee. Kneel in a crawling position with your hands palm down. Bend your knees to move your buttocks back toward your heels and stretch your arms forward.

- Shoulder Stretches:

  Stand next to a wall. Slowly "walk" the fingers of one hand up the wall, so that you feel a stretch. Hold. Repeat with the other arm. Stand holding one elbow with your other hand. Pull the elbow and arm across your chest so that you feel a stretch. Hold. Repeat with the other arm.

- Hip and Thigh Stretches:

  Sit on the floor with your knees bent outward and feet together. Using your hands, slowly press your knees down toward the floor. Hold.

stretching exercises. Stretching lengthens the muscles and gets them ready to work better. It also makes more blood flow into the muscles and joints, bringing in oxygen and nutrients. Ten or fifteen minutes of stretching will allow you to move and play better, and you will also greatly reduce your risk of injury. Often strains happen because muscles haven't been warmed up properly.

"No pain, no gain." You've probably heard that saying before. Some people think that to get a good workout, they need to lift and stretch until it hurts. That's not true. When you begin to feel pain, you've gone too far. Remember, pain is the body's warning signal. It's time to stop! You don't have to feel pain while you are exercising to get a good workout. You are working your muscles whenever you move your body.

Exercise Smarts

Every time you exercise, you are tearing muscle fibers. That's why you may hurt the day after a workout. It takes a day or two to heal. So it's best to exercise every other day or three times a week. If you exercise every day, then alternate: work one group of muscles one day and a different group of muscles the next.

Poor posture can strain your back muscles.

Do you slouch when you sit? Your shoulders may hunch or droop. Many people do this and don't even realize it. This is a sign of poor posture, and it can lead to strained back muscles. Sometimes, it seems hard to straighten your back when you are sitting or standing, but you actually use more muscles when you slouch. Then, the muscles have to work extra hard. If you try to keep your back straight, you are less likely to have back problems. See if you slouch during the day. If you do, remember to straighten your back.

Learning and practicing the best ways to sit, stand, walk, run, jump, and throw will lower your chances of being injured. And staying active will help to keep your body strong, flexible, and able to do whatever you want or need to do.

Glossary

analgesics—pain-relieving drugs

arthritis—pain, swelling, and stiffness of a joint

blood vessel—a tube that carries blood from one part of the body to another

bruise—an injury in which blood leaks from a broken blood vessel and collects under the skin

carpal tunnel syndrome—an RSI in the wrist, caused when swollen tendons in the narrow openings of the wrist bone press on the nerves. Pain and stiffness may develop in the hand and numbness in the fingers.

cartilage—the tough, rubbery tissue at the ends of bones

contract—to tighten

endorphin—a chemical released in the body that send "happy messages" to the brain

flexible—the ability to bend and twist

joint—bendable connections between bones, such as an elbow or a knee

ligaments—tough bands of tissue that hold bones together in joints

muscles—strong, stretchy tissues that pull on bones or other structures and move body parts

muscle cramp—an uncontrollable muscle contraction

muscle fibers—long, stretchy threads of muscle

repetitive strain injury (RSI)—damage to muscles, tendons, or nerve tissue as a result of performing the same action over and over while in an awkward position

skeleton—the bony framework that supports the body and gives it shape

tendon—a tough, cordlike tissue that connects muscles to bone

Learning More

Books

Feldman, Andrew. *The Jock Doc's Body Repair Kit*. New York: St. Martin's Griffin, 1999.

Garrick, G. James and Peter Radetsky. *Anybody's Sports Medicine Book*. Berkeley, CA: Ten Speed Press, 2000.

Griffith, H. Winter. *Complete Guide to Sports Injuries*. New York: The Berkley Publishing Group, 1997.

Micheli, Lyle J. *The Sports Medicine Bible*. New York: Harper Collins Publishers, Inc., 1995.

Micheli, Lyle J. *The Sports Medicine Bible for Young Athletes*. Naperville, IL: Sourcebooks, Inc., 2001.

Moffat, Marilyn and Steve Vickery. *Book of Body Maintenance and Repair*. New York: Henry Holt and Co., Inc., 1999.

Roberts, Robin. *Sports Injuries (Get In the Game)*. Brookfield, CT: Millbrook Press, 2001.

Organizations and Online Sites

Ankle Sprains

http://www.rice.edu/~jenky/sports/ankle.sprain.html

This site includes information on how to treat ankle sprains.

Human Anatomy Online

http://www.InnerBody.com/htm/body.html

This site provides educational and interactive views inside the human body so kids can learn more about their muscles, bones, and other body parts.

Kid's Health

http://www.kidshealth.org

This site includes information on many questions kids have about how their bodies work.

Questions and Answers About Sprains and Strains

http://www.niams.nih.gov/hi/topics/strain_sprain/strain_ sprain.htm

This site is provided by the National Institute of Arthritis and Musculoskeletal and Skin Diseases, part of the National Institutes of Health (NIH). A fact sheet gives an overview of sprains and strains including the difference between the two injuries, causes, symptoms, and treatment.

Sprains and Strains Are a Pain

http://www.kidshealth.org/kid/ill_injure/aches/strains_ sprains.html

This site, provided by kidshealth.org, has easy-to-understand information about strains and sprains, including a description, causes, and treatment.

What Are Sprains and Strains

http://www.mayoclinic.com/findinformation/condition-centers/invoke.cfm?objectid=F0138FF8-9AB3-4C66-A1FA2F6EFD7759F7

This site, provided by the Mayo Foundation, provides an overview of sprains and strains, including signs and symptoms, causes, risk factors, diagnosis, and treatment.

What You Need to Know: Sprains and Strains

http://www.health.com/health/wynks/Sprains_Strains WYNK2000_-MAL/whatitis.html

This site includes a description of the two injuries, as well as various links to further information, such as how to wrap an ankle joint.

Index

About the Authors

Dr. Alvin Silverstein is a professor of biology at the College of Staten Island of the City University of New York. **Virginia B. Silverstein** is a translator of Russian scientific literature. The Silversteins first worked together on a research project at the University of Pennsylvania. Since then, they have produced 6 children and more than 180 published books for young people.

Laura Silverstein Nunn, a graduate of Kean College, has been helping with her parents' books since her high-school days. She is the coauthor of more than 50 books on diseases and health, science concepts, endangered species, and pets. Laura lives with her husband, Matt, and their young son, Cory, in a rural New Jersey town not far from her childhood home.